NOT WHERE I WANT TO BE, NOT WHERE I WAS

~ A short memoir

By

Nisti K Delgroothe

This book is dedicated to those who are hurting, to those needing comfort, and to those who are trying to figure out next steps. May the LORD be your guide.

Acknowledgments

I thank the LORD God Almighty for salvation through Jesus Christ that allows me to share my secret with you, and for putting the many people in my life who helped make this day possible.

On this, my first publication, I thank everyone who helped make this day possible!

I thank my Mom and Pop, Paula and Melvin Kerr, for the expanse of their love and support–from my name, to "advisory meetings" at the kitchen counter, to tough questions to make me think, steadfast encouragement, and most of all, for loving me, especially during the really dark times.

I am thankful for my loved ones gone on. Their belief in me, love for me, and memory have never parted from me. They contributed to this day.

I thank…

…Liam's family for embracing me into the family and for your love and encouragement throughout the decades. You called me his "Rock"; he is the steel in my backbone, and my forever love! Thanks for sharing him with me! Joan, thank you so much for making this easier to tell! I love you all!

…my earthly shepherds throughout the years who brought the unadulterated gospel and who weren't shy to teach the need for repentance at the precious Throne of Grace. I am grateful for the sacrifices made by your family. You stay in my prayers and you've helped make this book possible! I hope you see that!

…my family for your love and support, expressed in so many wonderful ways that a separate book would be required! I love you! (Brother, thanks for always telling me, "Do your thing!")

…my spiritual family for catching me, lifting me, and keeping me propped up when my husband died. I can't thank you enough! I was sinking deeper than you know.

…my sister-friends for being with me through thick and thin! Each one of you has helped make this day happen in unique ways. Hugs and kisses! Love you!

…all whose hands helped shape "The House that Love Built" aka The Chateau on The Creek! Your craftsmanship is much appreciated and your friendship means so much to me!

…neighbor-friends who have embraced me, supported me, encouraged me, and helped me feel safe at home. I write, knowing you have my back!

…the brave man who faced a lion in the woods to make sure Binx and I were safe on my first writing retreat. We look forward to more adventures with you, but there might be tigers and bears!

…all those who helped care for me when I was sick. You didn't allow me to feel alone. Thank you doesn't seem enough. I write in good health, as God allows!

…all who helped shape and encouraged my writing career, from swapping stories as kids, calling me a "Writer" before I was ready, encouraging me to grow in the trade, mentoring me, and pushing me toward the mark called: My Best! I hope you are pleased as you see the fruits of your labors. LeAnne, big hugs to you!

…the famous people who took time out of their life, looked me in the eyes and said, "You can do it!", "Think BIG", "Just write!", "Tell the How! You've got it!"

…all who prayed for me. This day would NOT be possible if it weren't for you!!!

Most importantly, a special thanks to all who extended comfort to me. I hope and pray I am pouring back out what I have received! There are so many in need.

Reviewers, your commitment to excellence and requesting it of me is much appreciated! For you I am grateful! Thank you, Michael, Gene, Stephanie, Richard, and Loretta!

To my Mommy, you are the best technical advisor ever! I love you!

May God bless you all! ~ Nisti K

Introduction

If it weren't for the fact that I faced death many times, I would say I have always been the average girl, now average woman, who lives next door. On a good day I do my best to be a follower of Jesus Christ and take time to learn about Christ, God, and the world around me. The many lessons and observations that come forth stir my curiosities and leave me wanting more.

Tangibly, my life is pretty ordinary. I have a lawn to mow, a house to clean and maintain, and family and friends. I care for and enjoy the company of an eighty pound German shepherd by the name of Binx, so named because of exquisite canine characteristics. Her name evolved as I watched her sit on her hinds as a pup, a perfect canine specimen that looked more like a beautiful sphinx— motionless and exuding strength while watching the world with eyes that appeared lined with kohl.

If both my grandmothers' nine decades of existence were an indicator of my life expectancy, I would just be starting the "best years" of my life. Yet, I've been reminded no one knows their last days and I often question whether my reality is average when I hear people say, "You're so young" when they learn I am a childless widow.

Occasionally, someone will comment that my life seems interesting. I definitely believe it is! What people don't know is that I think a secret habit is the reason for the "interesting things" that happen in my life. I am not sure why, but I think it is time I let my secret out.

Yesterday

I had started calling my reflection and goal setting process a secret because only one friend besides my husband had been privy to hearing specifics about my year end indulgence. After I told my goal-oriented friend essentials of how I intensified my time with God in prayer, and how that led to specific goals about my entire life, I think he chose to forget.

My hush-hush tradition involved considerable time. It was, and would forever be, a demanding process. Over the many years of delving into the "hows", "whys", and "whens" of my goal setting routine, many people admitted they never set formal goals for themselves. Time was involved. Fail factors were involved. They were already involved in setting goals at work; they weren't interested in managing goals personally. "Why would anyone do that?"

Most people planned ordinary goals (even getting to work on time was a goal) but I met few who liked to do more than the ordinary. I watched people shudder at the thought of setting personal goals. I understood the anti-goal setting viewpoints and never tried to sway anyone otherwise. Nothing said ever left me thinking that I should abandon my practice.

Only two knew how I would peel away from the world and make plans for the year ahead. To others, I admitted being a goal-setter, but I didn't offer details. It had become like a sweet top-secret seclusion—less noise of the world and being more in tune with God.

Although I started the process in private prayer, the introspective thoughts and plans manifested afterward in quiet times and as I went about my daily routines. I could sit at a stoplight and have a goal come to mind. Just as easily, a critical insight might arise during dinner conversation. Prayer and Scripture served as the final confirmation of what I would pursue as a goal. *Owe no man nothing* rang out many times in my mind before my heart embraced the conviction to live that way. *"Love the LORD your God with all your heart", "Love your neighbor as yourself", Let your words be edifying, "Set your mind on things above".* All Scriptural principles to live by– some actual Scriptures, some paraphrases– that prompted goals in the year ahead.

I happily entered prayerful reflection and remained hopeful while drafting contemplative goals. I got used to doing both. It had become special time spent with my Maker and left me anticipating what He might do in my life. In time, it became easy.

Much of my career had involved helping individuals and businesses set goals to accomplish a task, project, mission, or vision, so goal setting was routine for me. My confidential process was borne from bits and pieces of my work, personal habits, and my spiritual walk. It had allowed me to see God work in my life as if my LORD was weaving a tapestry of my yesterday, today, and tomorrow.

~~~*"Many are the plans in a person's heart, but it is the Lord's purpose that prevails."* Proverbs 19:21 (NIV)

Journey

Life is different than I thought it would be. All its twists and turns leaves one word on my mind: JOURNEY

~Journey~

Stripped
Not for money
Stripped
Evil's joy
Stripped
Life's blows
You never know what a day will hold.

Stripped
Bare
Releasing
What you know
Covering self
Naturally
Clinging to what you dare hold.

Hands
Limp.
Core
Weary.
Like a babe
Curling
Close to a father's heart.

Changed
Destination
Starts.
Begins
With knowledge
Of heart.
Every traveler eventually knows a detour called:
The Restoration Road.

A Forgotten Find

I sat in my office where containers of paperwork, stacks of mail, and abandoned purchases surrounded me. Neatly lined bookcases flanked the room and spotlighted medical books, a classic literature collection, dictionaries, and an assortment of Bibles. The 1899 Bible Dictionary and the four inch International Dictionary deserved a shelf of their own. Atop a waist high bookcase a FedEx box containing an unfinished manuscript weighed down a papyrus painting that had curled. Finds gathered during world travels decorated the room. A floor model globe dared me to dream.

I pulled a sheet of paper from an old manila folder. On the left-hand side of the paper was a column for ACTION NOTES and on the right-hand side a column for PLANNING NOTES. The aged piece of paper was neatly titled in my hand's print: "1998 Goals". *Odd timing*! I read on. Under PLANNING NOTES was written: "Do more fun things". I chuckled at my priority. The second entry read: "Pay off my bills". I gasped and continued to read.

Beneath my two priorities of fun and no bills were five categories: mental, physical, social, financial, and spiritual. Under each category there were simply stated sentences; there were twelve sentences in all. In the ACTION section, I noticed names and phone numbers written in pencil. I am not sure why the names were there, yet, sixteen years later, each name evoked a face and story.

The first name written was that of a gentleman with whom I had a blind date. My coworker wanted us to meet and I agreed. I was a divorcee at the time—4 years to be exact. The gentleman and I had both studied Social Work and were around the same age. He was a professional athlete, handsome, and well mannered. We enjoyed dinner and live music on a double date with my co-worker and his wife.

Afterwards, my date mailed a card to me, expressing appreciation for the opportunity to meet me. A real gentleman! I think he wrote the card before a work assignment took him out of country. I don't recall why we did not get back in touch with one another. New phone number, new address, lack of interest? I don't know, but he was nice and I wondered what happened to him.

I Googled his name and his photo and bio popped up immediately. As I read his bio, I could not stop saying, "Wow!" The article detailed my blind date's career and all the local, national, and international honors he had earned along the way. Another article noted that he spent 16 years making a name for himself; and here, sixteen years after writing his name, I wondered how he was.

The second name was that of a gentleman who served the community as I did. We met at a conference, clicked, and talked for over an hour underneath the glow of the parking lot light. We both inched toward our cars until one of us brought up another topic that the other couldn't resist diving into with commentary or questioning.

Our conversation flowed effortlessly, from silly mundane things to serious topics like investigative work. We both dreamed of that. The last I saw him, he was getting ready for an interview and was excited and nervous. I encouraged him while we ate lunch. We parted, and I never saw or heard from him again. Googling did no good, and if he did get the job we both wanted, his picture would not be easily found.

The last name gently written was that of a woman I crossed paths with in my work. She hinted that I would be a suitable wife for her nephew. Her nephew never proposed and I married someone else. I saw her a few years ago while at a community event. We chatted and I had the feeling that things were going well for her. She wore stylish and brightly colored clothing that matched her lipstick, smiled throughout the event, and had sparkle in her eyes. I asked about her nephew and caught sight of a slight wrinkle on her brow when she said, "So, you don't know about him?" "No," I admitted.

I didn't dare pry for details. If details aren't offered, I seldom ask for them. I wasn't going to start then since the smile on my face was deliberate and could be in jeopardy. I politely lingered in hopes of an explanation, but my colleague never offered one.

Although the music and festivities were delightful, I occasionally wondered what I did not know about my colleague's nephew. Google results for my associate: she had risen to senior leadership for a private organization. Her nephew progressed in his career, too!

Seeing the names of these people written on my 1998 Goals felt and seemed providentially poetic. My memories of these people did not require stirring. They were established and professionally accomplished—at least 2 of the 3 could be proven to be. I, on the other hand, was just getting the strength and courage to start all over again. God had been restoring me through the darkest time of my life—widowhood—and now, four years later, it seemed I was gently being nudged toward a threshold of change.

In confidence, I told a friend during dinner that I was getting myself ready for the next phase of my life. My friend said they had never heard anyone refer to a change in life that way. I reconsidered my choice of words. Soon, I settled on their accuracy. My life had been full of drastic changes: losses, moves, and other unexpected occurrences. What I was facing in my future was not a matter of taking a few steps or entering a new stage. Much greater than that! Indeed, I was entering a new phase in a new life! Over seventy five percent of my life had been spent being a close friend and love interest of my husband who died tragically and unexpectedly. After dropping my career to follow his, after packing up and moving around the world with him, after losing him…none of what I was about to do was ever dreamed of, prepared for, or planned.

By nature, I tended to be a planner. Due to the severity of some of my health conditions after we were married, I had thought I would be the first to go. The first to die. In true nature, and in matter of fact ways when opportunities arose, I gently did my best to prepare my husband for life without me. Yet, here I was.

As I looked at my 1998 Goals I realized the first phase of a new life would call for concentrated effort and tremendous discipline. I would have many hurdles, and some of them were within my own mind. Grief and loss had pulled at the core of who I am, and like a police officer had slowed and blocked my flow—some of my most effective ways. As a result of grief, I had become disconnected with mental and physical processes that were once praised as "highly organized". My office showed so.

Truth Be Told

In the months following my husband's death, I had jokingly, yet seriously, given permission to friends to run an intervention if boxes and clutter didn't disappear from my tiny condominium. One friend asked if I had seen the show about people who hoard. I said I had not seen more than a few minutes of the show. No cable TV. My friend told me that the show pointed to traumatic events as the cause of what I was complaining about—being overwhelmed by things, piles of stuff and boxes, and a sense of disorganization. I still remember where I was when we had that phone conversation— sitting in my car, staring at my condo, suddenly wondering if I was in trouble.

The loft style condominium had been fully furnished like a hotel suite so my husband and I could rest easily when in town. In that capacity, it was comfortably spaced. As I started thinking about moving forward alone, I knew our lovely little place would be too small. My creativity had risen and I wanted a small studio for outlet and for income. Also, I had opened a flea market booth and the condo was barely large enough to embrace my inventory when I shut the booth down—not enough profit margin. The condo seemed as if it was ready to vomit when the movers brought some of our possessions from the rental we had been living in while in Michigan. It, too, was fully furnished.

The plan on the Michigan end was that some items would go into storage in Indianapolis, and food and personal items would go to our quaint condo in Indianapolis. Our residence in Michigan was roughly four times larger than our Indianapolis place of respite. The mover, who saw both places, listened carefully as I bravely directed where each box should be stacked. I didn't know how many boxes were coming. Eventually, he stopped and said, "Don't worry, Ma'am! I am going to leave a path for you. You'll be able to go upstairs when you need to rest." I think he could see through my robotic mask worn to get the job done. The cardboard box walls towered slightly over my head. Only a few boxes would be unpacked, and a few months would pass before my husband died.

Months after the funeral, I searched for a larger place — a new start with a studio. The first house was like a cute little blue and white box, and was down the street from the condo. It didn't work out—a mold problem along with repairs that exceeded my abilities and interest. There was a second house. It was a Lustron home design that left me fascinated, dreaming of the possibilities and special measures needed in its total steel design. It would be a sweet mental playground in which to settle! My realtor and I never heard back from the seller and the place remained vacant for a while. There was a third and fourth and fifth house seriously considered, many involving offers. All were places where I could get a fresh start and have room for Binx to romp, but something would not go right—a newly sprung leak, a silent or missing seller, or another person designated as the winning bidder. Friends prayed I would find a place; I prayed harder.

While frustrated at the sixth seller for allowing negotiated time to pass, I discovered the seventh house. I called Dorothy, my realtor, and told her what I found. Dorothy showed me house number seven the same day; it was vacant. Her tiny figure barely left the car before she started shaking her head in frustration and disbelief that fluid negotiations on house six had suddenly gone silent. It didn't make sense to her, especially since I offered what the seller wanted.

After going through house seven we went out back and my realtor stood on the deck, looked around, and said, "Oh my goodness! This is nice! This is it!" I smiled. I thought so, too, and knew that she wasn't simply saying so because she was tired of dragging me around town. The seventh house was it! Established neighborhood! An acre with my own little forest! A red brick house that had a creek out back! A basement workshop would become my studio! The closing was seamless and "the fastest" the closing agent had experienced.

I transitioned into the shell of a house. It had been stripped of almost everything except the toilets and built in shower and tub. The main bath was intact so I could work with the rest. As a little girl, my mother taught me that a lady should be handy with at least a hammer. And after starting our marriage in an apartment, my husband and I purchased a foreclosure that would teach us pleasurable and painful lessons about marriage, budgeting, home ownership, and restoring a house.

Most houses I had owned or co-owned became home sweet homes because of good ole fashioned sweat equity. Home ownership was affordable that way, but I knew it wasn't for everyone as I had learned the tough lessons firsthand. It was hard work and sometimes there was the unexpected. I had grown to be okay with all of that, if the neighborhood was to my liking.

Restoring a house alone, I knew that if I managed my budget correctly I could get help on the projects too big for me to tackle. Hard physical work would be ideal for me now. I needed it! Besides, the neighborhood had seemed friendly and there were plenty of low traffic streets where I could safely walk Binx. I had been nervous about leaving the condominium community that felt like home, not only because once inside our place you had the sense of being secluded in nature, but also because neighbors watched out for one another and displayed a true sense of community. A wise friend consoled and reminded me that God already had the next place in mind and that I would be just as comfortable there. When I started working on the house I told her she had been right!

As I started making my red brick house a home, I also enjoyed great conversation with the workers who came and went (some even became friends). Soon I called my house: "The House that Love Built" because I noticed something special happening there. I had prayed for a place that would lend to my healing and restoration. I was having more pleasurable moments, and when others visited or worked there, they seemed to be in a pretty good mood, too!

Everything didn't stay perfect for the mood. One month after purchase, my basement flooded. I thought of the gentleman who had done some of the plumbing in the house. There had been a lot of plumbing work so I had become comfortable with him. My brother-in-law had introduced the plumber to me and said he trusted he would help if other things were needed down the road. It was barely down the road time, but I was in a panic. I had replaced a sump pump before but not in the midst of standing water. *Would I get shocked?*

Frazzled, I called to see what I should do. I scooped up buckets of water, ran them up the basement stairs, and tossed them over the deck railing until my plumber-friend arrived. I told him boots were needed, but he went downstairs without his. It seemed he underestimated my advisement because I heard him say in a higher pitch than his voice, "Ohhhhh, I see what you mean!" I pictured ice cold sump pump water rushing over and into the side of his work shoes. I failed at stifling a giggle. The water pumped from the basement was crystal clear, and being around this nice man made it apparent that one day my heart might open to male companionship again. The house continued to emerge as a special place and I could feel and sense God restoring me, and refreshing others.

In my red brick house I watched the mailman and neighbors wave and chat with each other. Wildlife visited the grounds often and left me sighing from its beauty. I introduced myself to neighbors, and some of them told my family that they would keep an eye out for me. I discovered many of my neighbors already knew some of my family and friends. People said my new home looks like me.

The massive deck out back, wrapped with private woods, became a place of conversation, sweet distraction, and unexpected naps for myself and others. I experienced my first hummingbird visit there, captured pictures of a baby raccoon emerging from a den near the creek, and watched an adult raccoon napping on a tree limb. A black and brown butterfly landed on me over forty times and took my breath away. The sights and sounds of nature entertained me.

In spring, I began a daily habit of grabbing my first cup of coffee and reading God's Word amidst nature. A green bistro set on the upper deck became my favorite reading spot. As I watched nature bustling in daily affairs, it almost seemed like a message that I, too, needed to begin getting busy with my new life. The daily habit in Scripture stirred my restoration and left me smiling and content in my relationship with God. In a sense, the woods that wrapped around me during my private time mirrored what it seemed God was doing to me, wrapping me in His love and getting me ready for this new life as I walked through and endured grief.

I enjoyed working hard on the grounds and had a vision of what they would look like one day. I had a part time job that had gone from being "one of the most stressful jobs in my life" to a job I enjoyed as training grounds for my own shop in the future. I discovered a fox den and other beauty in my neighborhood while out on walks with my dog. I savored sweet memories of the new friends found here—workers who became friends and neighbors who became friends. I was moving forward. Financially, I worked within a tight budget to be a good manager of my money. I saw God's hand upon my life with not only people who helped me with tasks, people who rushed to help in emergencies, but also in the items that helped restore the house.

Timing had been perfect in finding new bathroom cabinets donated to a reuse store and sold at a discounted price. At another reuse store, pure cherry kitchen cabinetry was unloaded from the donation truck right before my eyes. I rushed to the front of the store and gave the sales clerk my name and told her as soon as the pieces were unloaded, counted, and the price determined I would pay her. The carpenter who became a friend gawked when some of the measurements of the cabinets fit the lines that had already been drawn on the walls. Only thing: none of us marked those walls. Perfect fit!

Despite the savings and found discounts, I still needed to tighten the financial reins. I had been looking for full time work, but doors weren't opening. I took on special projects, moved storage items into my house to save money, and returned to selling flea market booth inventory for extra income. My work reputation was solid and most employers stated the doors would always be open for me, but nothing was coming through. I worked hard on my new home, worked hard on the grounds, and worked hard at emptying boxes. I worked so hard that as soon as I laid my head down at night I was asleep. It was perfect that way! Little time to think.

One day, I woke up in the middle of the night with excruciating pain in my right arm. I rubbed it down with a pain reliever and thought little more of it. The same excruciating pain returned days later when I picked up a small bottle of water. That week at work, while reaching up for a rack above my head, I choked when it felt as if someone had pierced my shoulder with a searing red hot sword and retracted it with abandon. My boss, nearby, mentioned that trouble like mine was typical for people on our team. A visit to the doctor became necessary.

"Classic case of tennis elbow. Give it about a year to heal."

"What?!"

I couldn't believe the doctor's word or the time involved. I didn't have that kind of time? Obviously, I would have that kind of time as signs of tennis elbow appeared in both arms. I entered physical therapy but lost my part time job. I was grateful that God had made provisions for me in many ways. One way of provision was piercing me to action with His word long ago. The Scripture about not owing people had drawn me toward a debt free life.

Before then, I had gotten used to having a lot of bills. A thin and excitable coworker helped me with my financial sight one day. She walked into my office while I was taking a break.

"Whatcha doin'?"

"Taking a break. Paying my bills," I said as I turned to look at her.

"Girl, those are your bills?"

I turned back and looked at my desk. I hadn't left case files out only my bills.

"Yes, these are my bills."

"Oh pleeeeease, put those away. It is making me a nervous wreck to see all those bills. I can't believe those are all bills!"

I pushed the letters and statements aside, chatted with her briefly, then got back to work. My co-worker's shock and dramatic display over a stack of bills stuck with me. When I later read Romans 13:7 and 8 about paying what we owe someone and leaving no debt outstanding except love, it made me rethink debt. I began to think about life without long term debt. I began to think about owing no man anything, except payment for services rendered in the month. That is how the 1998 goals came to read: "Pay off my bills". Scripture had pointed to my ability to have a different life. I wanted that.

It would take many years to reduce my debt because my bills were stacked pretty high. Diligently, I reduced my debt. When I married my husband a second time, I showed him how to reduce his debt, which became our debt, and together we paid it down and built savings. That was then. Now, with this unexpected injury, I knew bills might pile. I had no health insurance and the money making projects would be delayed. There was no prospect of a full-time job. Not yet. I took it one day at a time. Unexpected checks arrived in the mail and I paid down bills with tears of gratitude in my eyes. I looked out at the woods in the back and wished money occasionally grew on trees. I had a lot of trees.

The Other Side Of The Story

One day at a time I faced my reality—injury, widowhood, growing debt, hospital bills, and no sign of a job. My morning time in prayer and reading pages between Genesis 1:1 and Revelation 22:21 helped me from falling apart as they encouraged me, strengthened me, guided me, and gave me hope. House shopping and transitioning had accompanied dark times in grief.

I was not new to having faith in the LORD God Almighty. My faith had grown, and seemed challenged to grow daily. My trust had grown, but I had been through so much for so long I felt worn and fragile. Like a babe needing comfort, I sought out my Heavenly Father. A Scripture I read gave way to precious imagery.

"He tends his flock like a shepherd: He gathers the lambs in his arms and carries them close to his heart. He gently leads those that have young." Isaiah 40:11 (NIV).

I longed to be this close to my Heavenly Father, close to His heart like a little lamb being held. My husband's embraces had always transferred my thoughts from woes, and I knew his comfort would be no comparison to my God's! I closed my eyes. I meditated on being close to my Maker. I meditated on the beat of His Heart and feeling the rhythms of His Breath while being carried close. I grew still and there was no thought other than of my LORD!

In reality, I knew I could not touch God. I had read in Scripture that no man could even stand sight of the immense radiance of His glory. When photographing the sun, I had accidentally dropped the shield from my eyes on occasion. My eyes retreated every time.

Being the case, how much more intense must God's radiance be if He set the sun in its place?! How could I be carried close to His heart? Literally, an impossibility! Spiritually, the vision offered a sweet abandon into a promise of a loving and intimate relationship with God. Practically, I strategized on drawing closer. God had left His word and Jesus had left the Holy Spirit for reason. I would do my best to find closeness in prayer, in His word, in meditation on Him, and in learning to "hear and see" the Holy Spirit's leading. When asked how I was doing, some heard me say. "I am well because I am in my Heavenly Father's Lap!"

It had taken years before I would have such a heart for Jesus, My Savior, and any semblance of a relationship with God, My Heavenly Father. It started slowly and surely, long ago. I had been a church goer way back to the times when squirming in hard wood pews followed threats of getting pinches "if you don't sit still!" I remember those younger days in church, just like I remember sitting alone in other wood pews when I got older. One day, listening to a story about Jesus, I started yearning to know more about Jesus the Christ. A handsome man would be used to take my yearning to a different level.

I was at my favorite place, the library, when I saw him. I had had a crush on him in my younger years and our families socialized on occasion. His deep dark eyes and chiseled face was recognizable. He seemed to recognize me, or so I hoped. I asked about his family members by name. We briefly got caught up on each other's lives, then, he asked me was I saved. "Umm. What do you mean?"

He asked if I had time to talk. *Talk to him? Heck yeah!* I was surprised when he pulled out a Bible. He explained how God is so holy that sin separates us from God and that is why Christ came, died, and rose again to reconcile us back to God. Never one to get into too much trouble, well, not the really bad, bad stuff...I defended myself as a church goer and one who knew about Jesus dying for our sins. Our sins.

"How is your relationship with Christ? Is he the Lord over your life?"

I didn't really know how to answer. Better yet, I couldn't believe this handsome guy pulled out a Bible... and was Bible deep in discussion with me. Nor, could I believe we were sitting in my car talking about Jesus. He continued.

"If you declare with your mouth, "Jesus is Lord," and believe in your heart that God raised him from the dead, you will be saved. That is what it means to be saved."

I did not know what to say. I listened more than I talked. The whole situation left me stunned. We were both single, and he was talking to ME, and talking to me about the BIBLE? After conversation back and forth and him flipping to Scriptures and reading them, he encouraged me to grow in my knowledge. He mentioned a few churches and then we said our goodbyes.

I couldn't believe I ran into him out of the blue. I hadn't seen him in over a decade. It seemed really weird, and I couldn't stop thinking about it. *Was I saved?* I don't know how much later it was, but one day on the hard, wood pews I listened intently to a story about Jesus. My heart was full of appreciation as I listened to how Jesus reached out to people, talked to them, and helped them. Yet, there seemed so much more to Jesus. I did not know what it was. Despite listening, something moving on my face drew my attention.

I reached up, touched my cheek, and caught a rolling tear. I had not felt before such a passion to know Jesus. My deep longing to know Jesus the Christ would not wane. I longed to grow in my relationship with Christ and tried out a few churches my handsome friend had named. It would not be long before I declared Jesus as My Savior, dying for MY sins and Lord over MY life!

The more I learned about my Holy God, Jesus my Savior, and the Holy Spirit, the more I realized I had a lot to learn. I started studying the Bible more, and my habit of praying changed. I talked to God in prayer more often. I had heard about the Bereans of ancient days who checked Scripture to see if what the apostle Paul said to them about Scripture was true. I studied so I could be more like the Bereans.

One year, after celebrating Christ's birth, thoughts of how I used time turned into deep reflection. Consideration of the passing year seemed more than appropriate and began to feel like a logical act of thankfulness for my life. I asked myself questions. *What did I do with the time allowed? What do I need to do better? What do I want to do better? What do I want in my life?* I had wondered if I had been wise in using the years God gave me. A few near death experiences had turned my thoughts to "Why am I here?" from time to time. Decembers rolled around, again and again, New Year resolutions drifted away into nothingness, and I was still living for a reason. I asked God to reveal what could be improved in my life. I scanned the passing year's activity calendar for my "Done" and "Not Done" tasks to see what I had committed to.

As I thought about who I was as a follower of Christ, the full picture of my life underwent reflection. Borrowing from my education and career, I broke down my life into segments: spiritual, mental, physical, and social parts of my being. I expanded those dimensions when it seemed, after praying, that there were more areas of my life that I might need to address such as my finances. Each year, I would enter a reflection period. Each year, I would write out my priorities and goals. As I started reflecting on the goals I had set, I began to see how God had been working in my life, not only through the goals that rose in my heart, but how along the road to completing those goals He worked in ways unimaginable. Reflection became an automatic process I entered into, and so did the goal-setting. When I married my husband again, I carried that habit into our relationship.

Until Death Do Us Part

Memories. We met as teenagers. Worked at the same job. On our first date we went to a park and talked as we strolled along a trail that headed into the woods. He walked in front of me. Suddenly, he flung his arms wildly and made loud noises. My flight instinct kicked in and I pivoted to sprint. He stopped me just in time, and it was then that I saw the massive spider web beside him as he pulled parts of it off his clothes.

During our first slow dance I told him, "I'm stuck on you." He said, "I'm stuck on you, too!" I hesitated, but had no choice but to destroy the moment. "NO,...I'm really stuck on you", I said as I pointed to my earring caught in his sweater. Our relationship would be full of laughs.

He took me to my prom. His first gift to me was Lauren eau de toilette (cologne) and… eau de parfum (perfume). Said he wasn't sure which was best so he bought them both for me. Always wanted me to have the best.

We dated on and off. Married. Divorced. Fussed about who the other was dating. Stayed the best of friends. We sat on a log and watched the sun set across the ocean. It all seemed right. Natural. We married each other again.

That summed up the stages of my relationship with a man named Liam who captured my heart and seemed to pronounce his love for me to the world. The second time around both my husband and I knew Jesus better, and had grown in our walk with him. While unpacking boxes as his widow I found a letter Liam had written. We had recently reunited in marriage, but we had not merged households yet. I had apparently been frustrated about something that happened and openly complained. In red bold typeface Liam addressed me:

My Dear Nisti,

I just got off the phone with you and realized how tough a person you are. I know how hard this separation is on you, but you are making the most of it by going over your boxes and getting rid of the items you don't need. I know the sacrifice that you are making and will be worthy of your love by my day to day actions. I will be the hardest working and most loving husband that you expect and deserve. I ask that you focus on the short term goals and block out Satan's negativity. Our reunion is a slap in the face to that being and he will try his best to make us stumble. Through our determination and desire to make each other happy we will take all obstacles and throw them back to the pits of hell. Don't focus on the separation, but rather focus on the things you need to do to come out and be with me.

Your Loving Husband, Liam

Liam had repeatedly encouraged me to keep my eyes on the LORD's bigger picture in our life. He had often reminded me the enemy was not all too thrilled about a couple who married, divorced, and reunited under God. Occasionally he deemed us to be in spiritual warfare. He was right.

Spiritual warfare would rise in our lives. Battles seemed a little easier when we recognized what was behind some of the stupid things that tried to pull us apart. Often times, the spiritual battles would intensify while he was away fighting a war on Middle Eastern terrain. The intensity of my prayer life rose then. I learned to trust God more, and in different ways than before. I continually prayed about my husband's safety. There would be too many close calls for comfort.

I got used to being away from Liam for a year or more, but when he came home it was as if he had never left. We labored to stay united. Both of us were reconciled to God through Christ and some disagreements were settled, standing on that common peaceful ground under Jesus. My husband made me feel as if I was a princess; I treated him like my royalty. Some asked, "Are you newlyweds?"

The last time Liam came home from combat, I began to have a battle of my own. Health challenge after health challenge beat down on me in succession. I was glad Liam was there, but knew he didn't need the stress. His new job was considered a high stress field. Yet, he was excelling.

Lovingly, Liam endured my illness related battles with compassion and suffered my health related crankiness with grace. I set annual goals to be a better wife to him, find work, and do what I could about my health. Something caused a spiral.

While I was fighting lingering health annoyances and isolation from unemployment, Liam started having a battle too. One day, he came home and stood by the fireplace. He had lit a nice low fire as he usually did on chilly nights. Our favorite show would soon be on and I told Liam we should get ready to learn a dance move. We would always reenact something on the dance show, something way beyond our skill level. Truth be told, we didn't have a skill level. We just had fun and enjoyed a good laugh recreating dance moves. It was a favorite in our week and he was always eager for the challenge.

This time, when I told Liam about the show coming on he stood on the red clay tiles next to the fireplace but didn't move. He stared, looking away from me, toward the wall, and didn't seem to hear me. He mumbled something over and over. Although I saw him standing before me, all my senses detected he was hundreds of miles away. He was not looking at me. He could not hear me. He talked as if in conversation. It was the first sign that he was fighting a new and bigger battle of his own.

I began to think of our illness related changes as monsters. My monsters formed as a result of damaged organ systems struggling for order; they flung intense emotions without warning. I wasn't sure, but it seemed Liam's monsters formed through trauma in days past. His monsters took him away. The monsters of our individual battles pulled at us, partnered with other monsters, and threatened our united front in marriage.

Emotionally, mentally, and physically we both endured battle related blows and grew weary. Spiritually, I was needy and stayed in God's word for strength; highlights and underlining in Liam's Bible suggested he did the same. I would seek the help of specialists and even be cut on (surgery); Liam would see specialists too.

One of my monsters weakened from radiation, another of my monsters was weakened by Liam's love. I wanted to believe one of Liam's monsters was crushed by my love, but privately, I was scared I had accidentally fed one. The struggle to hold onto ourselves, each other, and our marriage intensified. Our traditional and cheerful glad-to-be-home greetings dimmed. Eventually, there would be time apart in which we both reached for healing.

I prayed my husband's monsters would be slayed and he would be restored. Treatment started working for me. I had better days, and maintained hope for Liam. I sensed God doing something in my life. God seemed to be answering our prayers as the same seasons came and went. There would be one step forward and two steps back some days.

Fall, Liam's favorite season, had come again. The leaves were a vibrant array of reds, greens, golds and browns. I entered church for Sunday worship service, and found a seat in the middle section of the church. Suddenly, I realized I had not turned off my phone. I usually do that before entering the building so I quickly reached in my purse so I wouldn't be "the one" whose phone alerts sound off at the wrong time.

After service I said my goodbyes and walked down the sidewalk toward my car. I noticed an unusual amount of missed calls on my phone. I got in my car and returned one call. I did not feel sensation as I started slamming my open palm against the steering wheel. I heard the thuds and my voice yell, "No! No! No!" My sprinter's legs felt more like logs as I got out of the car and headed toward the church. I had no destination in mind, I was just moving.

A woman asked, "Is she okay?"

A church elder asked me, "Sis, what's wrong?"

I found breath in my body, drew on it, and told them Liam had shot himself and had died. A snatching sensation overwhelmed me, as if a firehose was being reeled in at warp speed. The hose was looped around a spot in my body, a spot representing oneness in marital union, a spot that could not be severed so it was taking me too. I physically began to sink. Arms caught me. I wailed. Voices rose in prayer while the circle around me grew. My pastor joined the circle. Bodies around me trembled. I screamed, "Satan did not win! Satan did not win!" All else I remember is that the heavens above seemed brilliant and bright blue.

Like a robot I tended to my husband's final affairs. Shifting my eyes from a stare took great effort. *"Come near to God and he will come near to you"* echoed in my mind. I drew closer to God and His word so that I could move. I searched every account of "widow" in the Bible and read the words for guidance.

I declined the pharmaceuticals offered, and kept noticing Bible passages that discouraged being consumed by wine. As a helping professional, I knew the way through pain and grief is to gently and steadily move through it. I did my best, but it was excruciating.

The television was on for noise. I didn't really watch it. An announcer's voice and words shifted my eyes from watching the flowing creek waters out back. I focused on the television screen. The announcer reported opening day of a movie in which I had landed a job as an extra. The date? The movie would open the day before Liam's funeral. Was this another of God's timing perfection to keep me from sinking? Was this a timing perfection to keep all who loved Liam from sinking too low to catch our breath? Tears streamed down my cheeks. I did not think they would stop. A week after Liam's funeral, family and friends took me to see the movie. I was visible. Nieces and nephews were excited! I sat in disbelief. It became a morsel of happiness for heavy hearts. It became a "rock" of remembrance of God's hand upon my life. Coincidence? Not this precise!

As days and months progressed, I heard more and more accounts of couples that battled like my husband and I had. It seemed radio and TV reports were timed alongside my best moments and revealed stories that would toss me into some of my worst memories. Men would share tales of their spiral into battles like my husband's stare; and I would find a boxed item that reminded me of our best moments, leaving me staring into a world of memories.

My emotions were up and down. My grief was heavy. I wondered if I had loved my husband enough. I grew tired of telling businesses he was gone. I hid behind widow's garb (no frill gray and black clothes), used lip gloss only as prevention from chapping, and continued to wear my wedding ring. The little things—opening mail with his name, getting dressed, shopping for one—required energy that I didn't have. I was tired, yet God's word was so powerful and faithful it became my sustenance like daily bread.

Boxes were still stacked and unopened. Over the first year of widowed life, mentally, and in my journal, I recorded special moments as if I had been watching a little child accomplish firsts. Natural smiles. Realizing I had closed my eyes and danced to a gospel song. Hearing a friend say they were happy I got my giggle back.

There would be forward progress and backward movement over the first three years as a widow, yet, God's care for me had been constant and faithful each day. I encouraged others having a difficult time that I would "move over" as there was plenty room to sit close to Our Heavenly Father's heart! The more I said those words, the more I started thinking to myself that one day the LORD might want me to get down from His lap, be helpful, do something new, and maybe even be a help mate to someone again. I didn't like the thought of getting away from the closeness I began to feel. I wondered why I would dare think I would ever have to.

The Choice To Return

As a widow, I had been spending quality time with God through prayer and meditation. Almost every day. Despite my daily habits, after finding my 1998 goals, I knew I needed to get back into my secret habit for life's next steps. When I found my 1998 Goals I was struggling. I struggled to plan my tomorrow. Honestly, I struggled with the day to day. It would seem natural that I would have turned to the respite of hopes and dreams, but there was only a trail of baby steps instead of a leap into what was sound.

In my initial widowed state, daily goals such as just get up and get dressed dominated my mind. In time, other short term goals emerged such as wrapping up Liam's affairs, and managing to-do lists that demanded attention. Shortly after Liam's death, I attended a succession of other funerals, including my physician's and the loved ones of family and friends. Due to demand, I returned black dresses to the front of my closet, instead of the back where I had gotten them. Life had never seemed so short. Seven deaths in ninety days left me thinking that life was meant to be lived fully, even now by me. I started moving forward in my life, but was limp from disorganization and a struggle for consistency. The lists I robotically managed were training grounds that would prepare me to make life changing goals once again.

A found notebook page with "DISTRACTION STOPPERS" written at the top suggested that I had at least thought about my goals at a deeper level. "Set 2013 Goals!" was listed on the page along with categories of "Writing, Spiritual, Personal, Social, Emotional, Mental / Intellectual". Returning to my habit occurred in small steps.

It would prove to be more than a notion. In fact, I don't think I sat still long enough to really enter the process at its fullest. That is, until I got sick.

I caught a cold. I quickly nursed my cold in all the ways I knew would keep it at bay—increased hand washing, vitamin C, chicken soup, more water, extra rest, and staying away from sneezers and coughers, or at least holding my breath until I could get away from them. My cold subsided in two weeks, then, after a brief and false sense of health, my chest tightened. I had learned years before that it could be a potential sign of bronchitis. I tended to myself and did everything I knew to keep the upper respiratory thingy from becoming something more—chicken soup, mint tea, rest, making sure I was covered up to my neck, and not going from extremes in temperatures indoors to outdoors.

My ward off attempts usually worked quickly, thoroughly, completely, and successfully. Despite having had health challenges in the past, I ran away from illness with prevention and quick intervention strategies. I often said I didn't have time to be sick, and seldom was. Long ago, I had been drawn to build health goals which not only helped improve conditions present then, but also the frequency of colds and viruses. Not this time! I felt better for a week and then I found myself in Urgent Care. I bundled up head to toe, struggled to breathe, and felt guilty for doing so. My classification: a walking germ factory.

After meds and return home, a soaring temperature rushed me back to doctor's care in two days. Test results: I had the flu. Flu? I don't get the flu! To my knowledge, I had not had the flu as an adult. The flu-induced horizontal posturing left me fussing that I was lying around being unproductive. I decided, instead of doing nothing, it might be a good time to enter into the reflection period I had known was necessary. *I decided?* When the flu symptoms didn't drop me to sleep, I prayed and thought of my life. Sometimes I blew my nose because of the flu, sometimes I blew my nose because of the tears that flowed from reflection. There was so much change needed in my life. *Where should I start? What should I do?* That became the basis of my prayers.

It was the first time since widowhood that I spent considerable time in prayer, dissecting my life. The use of sick time might have been a reflection boot camp of sorts. I had gotten rusty. Maybe I wrote goals and maybe I didn't. If I did, the goals were still being held hostage, most likely beneath piles of papers.

When I found my 1998 Goals, I eagerly looked forward to the process and its benefits. Yet, I was still busy managing daily affairs and juggling to stay on top of work projects and service activities. Although I was struggling, I was feeling stronger emotionally, was more productive, had a budding social life and felt my spiritual life was sound. The sense of closeness to God had always been the most pronounced pleasure of my practice; it felt like my life had been offered up in worship. I was not perfect in my sometimes humble walk with the LORD, but I felt my relationship was solid. Daily reading and meditation was powerful! The goals could wait; I was O…K. As a result, I made excuses and delayed starting the rigors of my in-depth time of thought. One of my workout goals and a patch of ice helped redirect me.

Rushing to and fro was a bad habit of mine—a sign of cramming all I could in a day. I hurried off to Bible Study at lunch and never saw the three foot patch of ice just around the side of my red Jeep. My body jerked and advanced in S movements like a freshly moved Slinky toy. I thought nothing of it, except that I hadn't seen that coming! Off I went. That night would be the first night of my Ballet Barre class and I rushed off to it too, not slipping though, but "dewing" more than I expected from foot pointing and body posturing near the barre I had grown to miss. Intense workout! My body appreciated it and the soreness returned my thoughts to the "No pain, No gain" mantras in earlier years.

In the days ahead, sitting at my home office desk became uncomfortable. Eventually, when I had to lie flat on my couch to endure a teleconference, I thought I'd better check with a doctor. Once again, my busy lifestyle would be halted.

"Bend over."

I did.

"How far can you usually bend?" the tall blonde Orthopedics doctor asked.

"I can usually touch the floor."

"Oh, I better check x-rays," she declared.

I sighed, slowly curled my body back up, then tried to keep pace with the technician taking me for an x-ray. I gave up. I hurt. She realized she'd left me and slowed down.

"Well, nothing is broken. You've strained your neck and back pretty good! I'm ordering physical therapy and muscle relaxers," said the doctor after the x-ray results came in.

"Thank you," I said, doing my best to create signs of appreciation on my sullen face.

At home, lying on my back, in and out of the first adjustments to a muscle relaxer, I thought more about my life ahead. Needing to feel as if I was productive, I grabbed a notebook and pencil, prayed, and jotted down what came to mind. I had never been too technical with the breakdown of my goal categories: Spiritual, Physical, Social, Mental, and Emotional. They were aspects of my humanity, helped give thought to my entire existence during reflection, and were aids to thought flow when setting goals.

Under "Mental/Intellectual" I included goals about the health and productiveness of my mind—thoughts, new learning, and overall mental health. Under the "Physical" category, maintenance and improvement upon general health of my body was considered. "Social" goals involved my interaction with others. "Emotional" was all about feelings. In my vocation we used to communicate them simply as "mad, sad, glad, and scared." Someone once mentioned they didn't like the variety of meanings of mad: intense anger or insanity. I didn't mind staying with the word mad, either definition fit.

When thoughts lingered around my next steps for employment, I added "Professional" as a category. "Spiritual"— the permanent category—involved building my relationship with God. "Financial" and "Environmental" necessities rose in thought and became other groupings. I thought my categorical divide was always thorough—not too much and just enough.

I was overwhelmed by the outpouring of need-to-dos surfacing under each topic on my list. Not wants, but needs! In over twenty years of extracting life's next steps in prayer, I had never had a list so long. As I thought about it, I had never before been a widow either. The list made sense. I was transitioning. I reviewed my brainstorm then prayed about what I saw.

Soon, I scratched off, rearranged, and circled items as commonalities formed. A shorter, more concise list emerged. Trained in making goals specific, measurable, attainable, realistic, and time specific (SMART goal technique), I listed completion dates. I used "increase" or "decrease" as a measurement indicator on some goals. Bad habits, such as my sleeping habits, benefited from being measured as increases in new behavior. "Increase" and "decrease" wasn't the most specific measurement, but being too much of a stickler would result in less change. I had figured that out from previous years.

My 2015 goals appeared! I printed them on a clean piece of paper. They were now official! But, I was not finished! After setting goals from year to year, I began adding one final note for myself at the end: "Leave room for God!" I had hoped I was getting a little bit better about doing that!

A Work In Progress
Yesterday and Today

Over twenty years ago, when I first started setting goals through this process, I kept the goals on the Notes page in my planner. This time, since I lived alone, I neatly re-wrote my 2015 goals on stationery bordered with gold and white fleur-de-lis, slid the paper in protective plastic sheeting, and pinned the goals onto my office bulletin board. I had gotten rusty with my habit and it was important to keep action items near the forefront of my mind. Whenever I passed the decorative paper, it was a reminder of my commitment so I reviewed the twenty six item list to see what needed to be done.

Throughout the year I checked deadlines and what I needed to keep in mind. Occasionally, I set a 15 minute timer to make progress toward a goal. One of my friends laughed at my timer approach, but setting a timer for 15 minutes of pure focus and concentration worked wonders for me! Phone turned off. Pushed away from the Internet. Good tunes in the background! I would not stop until the timer said so. Ding! Progress!

I first used the technique long ago to organize an out of control linen closet. Timer set. Work, work, work. Times up! Bam! I couldn't believe how a time press produced such results! Since then, I have used that technique for everything from a quick exercise workout, to tidying-up the house, even to organizing paperwork to pay taxes. I used the same method to work toward a financial goal—a 2015 budget.

One day, I realized the deadline for completing my budget was near. I set my timer for a few minutes and listed all utility bills in my columnar pad—my budget log. (I've used the green pads so long that this type pad is what my co-worker saw gaping when she asked what I was doing, then panicked over my stack of bills.) I set my timer another day and gathered all non-utility bills and entered them in the log. Timer set. Another day. Another portion of the task done. Eventually, my budget was made in "stolen" moments!

I was glad to take a bright green highlighter and mark that goal off my list: "Budget before February 1, 2015." I was late, but had done it! An important fact was revealed. I had thought that in my hustle and bustle I was spending too much money on trivial things. And, I thought my medical bills had caused those big dips into my dwindling savings. They had, but they weren't the only cause of shrinking dollar signs. A significant monthly deficit was the culprit! How did I miss that? Had I been too busy to see that before now? Had I been shallow in awareness from grief? That was unlike me. Well…it was just like me. Now.

I did not need to pray about springing into action, but I did pray about finding the remedy! I needed more income! I tightened up with money-saving strategies: cancelling magazine renewals, planning errand routes so I didn't use as much gas, and taking advantage of rewards discounts. I found an ideal, take-the-assignment-or-turn-it-down-without-penalty type contract. When I felt well, I took as many assignments as I could. I met a lot of people! It was even a fun job!

Later, I would have to face facts and lay under a surgeon's knife. Two days before my surgery, I received a call from my former university. In my second to last class, Liam died during finals week, and I abandoned finals and dropped out of school. The school was calling to let me know that in an "unusual decision" made on my behalf, half of my remaining financial burden to complete my degree would be lifted! What?

A requirement was that I explain why I initially started the educational pursuit. Family was my reason, my husband's worry free transition into retirement was my reason. Answering that question stirred mixed emotions as I faced fallen dreams of supporting my man while repositioning myself in a life without him. I wondered about the call's timing. Returning to school was not a 2015 goal, but tackling "unfinished" things in my life was. I sat and thought about what had happened and what was happening. It seemed as if I had been prepped for a call from the school.

It felt like encouragement that only God could provide before I faced the surgeon and her scalpel! God knew my financial concerns. God knew some of my dreams were being buried. There would be no fruit from my womb. No full term pregnancies for me. No babies naturally. At one time I wanted six children.

It seemed the LORD was teaching me that sometimes I have to go back to go forward. Maybe even be stung by pain from the past. If I really trusted and believed, I needed to release dreams of the present and past, and surrender them to My LORD. If I really trusted and believed, I may need to pick up something I left in my past and carry it forward with me: a finished education. Revisit the past for benefit of the future!

As agreed, one week after surgery I started classes again. Anesthesia related brain fog set in and I was out of practice as a student. Energy hovering to heal the mark left by the surgeon raced past the scar line and became concentration! I had to calculate possibilities and process mathematical formulas in Quantitative Analysis! I had to plan a business from scratch, including its financials! Talk about tough! What had I been thinking?!

Along with the emotional mix, returning to school was not seamless. It had been unusually awkward and I sometimes questioned if I had processed the school's call correctly? *Isn't a faith step a smooth walk?* This one wasn't. My online student account froze during the syllabus review week. When it unlocked I barely had time to glimpse over all the documents, instructions, timelines, and assignments due. My planning time was squashed. I did my best to plan so I wouldn't fall behind. I was already working at a disadvantage since I had been out of school for years. Sure enough, I got behind anyway because I rushed past a one line sentence detailing an assignment. My stomach churned when the professor asked for the report I had not read about, nor had I prepared. My body tensed. I knew my body did not need that. I scrambled to catch up but wanted to quit. My grade point average was at risk. I had thought it an important re-entry stamp for the job market. Friends advised: "Just finish". I did.

I finished my degree with honors. *Honors?* I had never experienced such a level in my academic pursuits. In addition to that, I was excited about a newly discovered business skill, made known to me as a result of my last class. As CEO of a global company in an interactive business strategy competition, I, NKDelgroothe,Inc. ranked in Top 10 and Top 50 in the world, partially because of accurate industry forecasting. It was just a game, but it wasn't only a game! It was needed encouragement! Time would tell how God would use my new found skill as my future rolled out. Even though I was good at determining probabilities, I dared not guess; I'd get it wrong.

The morning after I finished degree requirements, I sipped coffee and thought about it all. My busy-body pace stopped for studies. That gave me time to heal. The budget had revealed a shortfall, and that knowledge led to a flexible job, earnings enough to pay off hospital bills and pay for my last class! The interweaving of tasks and goals, the past and present, my yesterday and today, it took my breath away! How God brought it together was remarkable! I poured myself out in thanks to God for ALL He had done! Every good thing was and is from God! The Bible says so!

Wrap It Up and Tie It With A Bow~ Reflection

December 2015. Almost a year passed since immersing myself into deep reflection, goal setting, and next steps. It took a lot of discipline, concentration, and faith. It wasn't easy, and I didn't always complete my goals on time. The lessons left plenty to think about the rest of my life.

Now, it was time to do it all over again. Pray. Reflect. Pray. Extract lessons and accomplishments. Pray. Set goals for the New Year. Pray. Have faith. Pray. Take steps toward goals over the next 365 days. And most importantly, leave room for God to intervene!

I removed my 2015 Goals from a stack of papers on my desk and scanned the yellow and green highlights, circles, and checkmarks that proved twenty (20) out of twenty-six (26) goals had been completed! I was still getting my "act" together, but God had seen to it that there was significant change in my life—a body rid of a diseased organ, a new degree and new found skill, and a creative studio nearly finished. There were other advances in the passing year, but there were also six goals that had not been met. I studied those. Goals regarding my finances, environment, and profession topped the list as needing more effort. My sole emotional goal had seen progress, but needed much more work. It was my most significant struggle and the biggest obstacle in completing other goals.

In my journal, I noted regret over "poorly spent time." Poorly spent time was a casualty of my emotional goal not being mastered. A Scripture came to mind that would help with that. I contemplated pulling out the calculator and estimating time lost, but I did not do it. Two days later, on New Year's Eve, my pastor's sermon would bring the point back home, as if I needed a stern reminder. As my pastor encouraged us to make three biblically aligned resolutions for the New Year, my jaw dropped when he said resolution number two.

"Resolution Number Two: Stop…wasting… time!"

Really?! I made faces during my pastor's sermon. As if I hadn't been convicted enough with my private declaration of wasted time, I had a roughly six foot two, two hundred some pound ex-college football player telling me to knock it off. I think I said, "Ouch!"

When I got home and looked at my 2015 Goals, I turned up nose and lips in a stink face as I realized what had suffered from my waste of time. It had been God's precious time I wasted anyway.

"I could have done that and that and that," I said, pointing to non-highlighted goals.

I crossed my arms and took a little walk. As I thought about the time drizzled away, I realized the greatest frustrations throughout the year involved time, but the haste of it. I had purchased a car too soon, missing its poor reliability rating. In school I had become too concerned on getting behind and missed an important detail. Missing that detail caused great stress.

In comparison, my best frame of reference on how my time should have been handled was my surgery. I had waited a considerable amount of time before deciding on surgery (years!) and did all I could for my health before progressing.

My recovery had gone well, even with a trapped nerve that screamed to be relieved. My doctor, who had walked in my room before surgery and reminded me "God is covering us!", had been cheered when I showed up to my post-surgery checkup wearing clothes and even wearing jewelry!

My surgeon had been correct! God had covered me during surgery, during my recovery, and during everything else in my year. (Or, so it seemed!) God's covering didn't mean I wouldn't have to work hard and do my best. It hadn't meant everything would be smooth as silk either.

While reflecting on my past year, my daily reading involved a Scripture that would help me understand more. The Scripture was about Jesus seeing the disciples in their boat, straining and toiling while at sea. Jesus didn't stop their struggle immediately. I lingered there in thought. I have been on a cruise liner in a storm. It was very scary! I was really surprised by Jesus' response until I thought of my days as an athlete. I was most developed after toil— pulling ankle weights daily to strengthen my runner's legs, running around the track repeatedly to build my endurance, lifting weights. Looking back at the tough times in 2015, those were times that built strength in me!

Here I was about to embark on a new journey in a new life. Here I was asking what I should do. And here My Shepherd was reaching out through my goals, through my prayers, and through my time with Him! He was encouraging me, His little lamb, to be eager for a future, but cautioning me not to operate in haste, while allowing me to labor so I might be strong. What a year! What an amazing year! It seemed most important to remember that My Shepherd had carried me throughout it all, even in my past, assuring me He would carry me when needed in my future! That Isaiah Scripture! The little lamb!

For me, it began to seem as if it might be time to get down from My Heavenly Father's Lap. I had learned so much while there, but I wasn't meant to stay there.

"He showed you, O man, what is good. And what does the LORD require of you? To act justly and to love mercy and to walk humbly with your God." ~ Micah 6:8 (NIV)

It has become one of my favorite verses and it came to mind during this process. Walk. Yes, it is time that I get down and walk on this restoration road, as there may be other little lambs that I am supposed to meet. Little lambs that need to know that they, too, can be carried tenderly through and past whatever injured them.

I had been such a worn and lame little lamb, and now my experience has helped me to "see" other lambs that might be limping. If I do encounter them and they ask my reason for smiling or having pep in step, I will show them the scar over my heart and tell them the story is already written.

2016 Goals soon started to flow!

~~~~~~ *** ~~~~~~

"Many are the plans in a person's heart, but it is the Lord's purpose that prevails." Proverbs 19:21 (NIV)

~~~~~~ *** ~~~~~~

~~Journey Poems~~

Throughout my journey a lesson learned or thought
harnessed rose as a poem or two. Here are a few:

~Past. Present. Future.~

I look up to the heavens,
the host of my future.
I gaze at the rhythm of the clouds.
No other place knows next steps,
unless I look down at the ground.

~

I fix my eyes there,
NOT the ground,
but where the sun shines bright
and clouds take new shapes every moment,
just like my future.

~

As the skies change before my eyes,
so does my present. I stop
and celebrate each moment, the people, the opportunities,
and the blessing found here
the right now.

~

For the present is all that IS.
I glance over my shoulder at the past,
only long enough to see
which steps caused pain.
I care not to step that way again.

~

I'd rather dance in the present
and sing as I raise hands
toward the sky!
My future!
Only known by One!

~ Restoration ~

I stand under the flow of rushing waters
O' how they cleanse and refresh me
Scrubbing off and away my yesterday
Leaving hope of eternity and tomorrow.

~ ~ ~

~~Scripture References~~

This section lists the Scriptures I referred to in this book. I wrote in the same way that I converse and think, where Scripture rises from heart and mind as a paraphrase or direct quote. I have done my best to share the Scriptures in order of their appearance in this book. Most of my reading is in the New International Version of the Bible (NIV), therefore, you might see slight differences depending on the Bible version you use.

I referenced the Bereans (Acts 17:11) who checked Paul's words against Scripture. If you like to be Berean-ish, you'll see I have noted when I paraphrased Scripture in the book. This list is not exhaustive of each occurrence of these Scriptures; some of these verses can be found in other books of the Bible as well.

"He tends his flock like a shepherd: He gathers the lambs in his arms and carries them close to his heart." (Isaiah 40:11)

"If you declare with your mouth, "Jesus is Lord," and believe in your heart that God raised him from the dead, you will be saved." (Romans 10:9)

"Come near to God and he will come near to you." (James 4:8a)

"Give to everyone what you owe them..." (Owe no man nothing paraphrase) (Romans 13:7, 8)

"Love the LORD your God with all your heart..." (Luke 10:27)

"Love your neighbor as yourself" (Matthew 19:19)

Let your words be edifying (paraphrase of Ephesians 4:29)

"Set your mind on things above" (Colossians 3:2)

"He showed you, O mortal (man), what is good. And what does the LORD require of you? To act justly and to love mercy and to walk humble with your God."(Micah 6:8)

~~~

~~My Secret Habit~~

Many people do not set goals; yet, many do. I, at the date of this writing, do not know of anyone who uses this same strategy for meeting with God over their passing year and the year ahead. Since many individuals do set goals, there are likely others setting goals in a similar way as I do, especially since the SMART goals technique and the areas of life are standard knowledge in the helping professions, business, and other arenas. However, what I have presented is my secret habit. I have enjoyed this habit more than twenty years.

I present my method in case you want to give it a try. Please see my tips below and adopt what works for you. If you are doubtful whether this works or will work, ask yourself if you believe this Scripture: James 4: 8. If you've decided to give this your best effort, here is how I suggest you proceed:

_Reflect and pray about your past year.

_Write down the main areas of your life: Spiritual, Social/Emotional, Mental, and Physical.

_Ask God to reveal the areas of your life that need your focus.

_Be open to God's answer!

_Write down any Scriptures that may begin coming to mind. Find Chapter and verse for them. If no Scriptures come to mind, you can look up Scriptures that relate to the areas of life. Search a Bible topical index for that.

_Under the appropriate area of life, begin to list what God brings to heart and mind. It might be tasks, behaviors, or specific matters. (Other areas such as Finances could be brought to your attention. See areas under SMART Goals).

_Note any specifics that come to mind such as increasing or decreasing, starting or stopping or completing.

_ The goal is to address what God brings to mind as needed change. Write down your goals as drafts.

_ Pray about the goals you came up with.

_ Make changes to the goals, if needed.

_ Finalize SMART goals (see SMART Goals), store privately, but where you can refer to your list regularly.

_ Pray about your list, your year, and what you are about to do.
_ Take steps to work toward your goals!

_ Periodically, document progress.

_ Thank God for progress!

_ Start all over again!

~~~

~~SMART Goals~~

You may have already heard of this acronym for setting goals. It is very common in many business settings. Basically, you develop goals that are specific and realistic. You don't want to set yourself up for failure. And, you'll want to know when you have completed your goal so it will need to be written in such a way you can measure your success.

You might want deadlines other than the end of the year. End of month, seasons, and special dates such as anniversaries or dates of birth can be motivating timelines used to complete goals. Most of us benefit from setting a date so we know and expect when we need to have something done.

Finally, set a goal you can achieve. Make sure the goal is attainable! Again, that is another way to set yourself up to win, not fail! That is it!

SMART—specific, measurable, attainable, realistic, time oriented. You might hear mention of slight variations of some of the acronyms letters. The principle remains the same.

Goal Categories - When considered as a whole, the aspects of a person's being can be broken down into categories of existence. Terms vary, but are primarily listed as those below in bold print. If you choose to try my goal setting strategy, please start with one of the five categories below.

Spiritual—related to one's spirituality in relationship with God.

Social—related to one's relationship and connection with others.

Emotional—related to one's feelings—mad, sad, glad, scared. (Often combined as Social/Emotional)

Physical—related to maintaining or improving one's physical health.

Mental—related to maintaining or improving one's outlook, behavior, and mental health.

In time, and as required, goal categories can be expanded to include other categories as needed.

Intellectual—related to improving one's education or increasing knowledge.

Environmental— related to the physical environment around you.

Professional /Occupational—related to one's job or occupation (how you make a living.)

Financial—related to how one's money is managed.

Please remember: one goal, and effort toward accomplishing it, can make a tremendous difference in life! More isn't better, so please don't feel the need to push for too many goals.

Be led in prayer!

~~***~~

NOT WHERE I WANT TO BE NOT WHERE I WAS

ABOUT THE AUTHOR

NISTI K DELGROOTHE lives in Indianapolis, Indiana with her German shepherd, Binx. She has other writing projects started—fiction and nonfiction—and looks forward to sharing them. Nisti K would enjoy connecting with you online. To follow or contact her online:

Twitter: @Nisti_K_News
Facebook: facebook.com/nistiknews

Notes

Notes

www.ingramcontent.com/pod-product-compliance
Lightning Source LLC
Chambersburg PA
CBHW071853020426
42331CB00007B/1985